GOLDEN HOMEMAKERS

Lots of gifts for you to make

Marshall Cavendish London & New York

CONTENTS

Our thanks to the following for the use of characters in the Collage. 'Peter Rabbit' and 'Sally Henny Penny' by kind permission of Frederick Warne & Co. Ltd; 'Dougal' © Serge Danot; 'Sergeant' © Gordon Murray; 'Mickey Mouse', 'Thumper' and 'Dumbo' ©Walt Disney Productions Ltd; 'Rupert Bear and friends' by kind permission of Beaverbrook Newspapers Ltd; 'Sun', 'Aeroplane' and 'Black Flower Cat' © Gallery Five Ltd.; 'Lions', 'Doves' and 'Owls' from Noah's Ark, a Paperchase paper designed by Cliff Richards; illustrations by Max Velthuijs by kind permission of Abelard-Schuman Ltd. And our thanks are due for all the other characters cut from many favourite books and cards by an enthusiastic child before identification could be made!

Edited by Liz Goodman

Published by Marshall Cavendish Publications Limited, 58 Old Compton Street, London W1V 5PA

© Marshall Cavendish Limited 1973, 1976

This material has previously appeared in the publication '65 *Easy to Make Gifts*'.

ISBN 0 85685 185 X

Printed in Great Britain by Petty and Sons Limited, Leeds.

Accessories by kind permission of	Photographs by
Asprey Ltd.	Camera Press
Bancroft and Partners	Steve Herr
The Carborundum Co. Ltd.	Chris Lewis
Craft Gallery	Maison de Marie Claire
Dolcis	Michael Murray
J. Floris Ltd.	Michael James Ward
Galts	
Habitat	Designers
Harrods	
John Lewis	Shirley Farrow
James Neill (Sheffield) Ltd.	Sally Goodyear
Olaf Daughters	Amanda Hanbury
Record Marples Ridgeway Tools	Alex Lloyd-Jones
Sanderson	Joan Reckitt
The Saturday Shop	Tessa Reuss
Stanley Tools Ltd.	Anita Skojld
	Gwen Swan

1

Lined sewing basket

Materials

½ yard 36-inch wide seersucker or printed
    cotton or gingham
1 yard cotton wadding
1 yard piping cord
Shirring thread
1 flat round basket, about 8 inches to
    9 inches in diameter, and 3 inches to
    4 inches high.

Making up

Cut circle of wadding to fit base and cut
strip, measuring circumference by depth of
basket for lining the sides and base.

Cut out circle of fabric for base of basket
and a strip to go round the inside.

Cut out two or three pieces for pockets,
each measuring depth of basket plus one
inch, by required width of pocket. Allow
½-inch turnings throughout.

Cut bias strip, 1¾ inches wide by circumference of basket. Join bias strip into a circle
to fit top of the basket and cover the piping
cord. Join the side strip into a circle and
pipe the top edge, snipping at intervals for
ease.

Turn in 1 inch on tops of pockets. Turn in
remaining raw edges and press. Gather tops
of pockets with two or three rows of shirring

thread. Position pockets on side and stitch
in place.

Place wadding lining in base and round sides
of basket. With right sides together join the
side strip to the base circle and place in the
basket over the wadding. Turn in seam
allowance round top edge and stitch round
the top edge of basket under the piping.
Stitch lining into position round base.

Patchwork needlecase

Materials
Scraps of cotton fabric
12 inches by 6 inches piece of cotton fabric for lining and 6 inches square piece for back cover
1 inch hexagon template
1 inch diamond template
Flannel for needles
Cardboard for front and back covers

Making up
Making the patches: Using the template, draw round with sharp pencil and carefully cut out the paper shapes.
Press fabric if creased, then using the template as a guide cut out the patches, allowing $\frac{3}{8}$-inch extra for turnings. Try to keep the two edges of the template parallel to the grain of the fabric as this strengthens the patch.
Pin the paper shape on to the wrong side of the fabric and fold over the turnings. Starting with a knot or back stitch, tack round the patch, using one tacking stitch to hold down each corner. Finish off by making a small extra stitch to hold down each corner and take out pin.

Joining the patches: Put the right sides of two patches together and oversew with tiny stitches along one edge.
Start by laying end of thread along top of edge and sew over it from right to left. Push the needle through fabric at right angles to edge so that stitches will be neat and patches will not stretch. To fasten off, work backwards for four stitches.
Make sure corners are firm by sewing extra stitches over them. Sew together small units first and join up these groups later when you can plan the finished effect to your satisfaction.

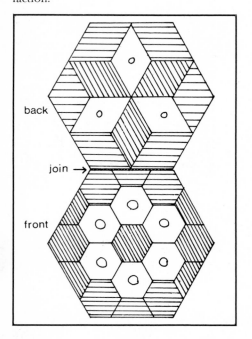

Using hexagonal template make up patches for front cover. Using diamond template make up patches and appliqué them to back cover of fabric. Cut cardboard into two hexagon shapes and cover the front and back pieces of card with your patchwork.
Cut lining into two hexagon shapes adding $\frac{1}{2}$-inch turnings. Line front and back, turning in raw edges and slip stitching together.
Oversew all round outer edge with contrasting cotton and sew back to front down one side of hexagon to form a book. Sew a folder of flannel inside and fill with needles.

Covered coathangers

Materials
Coathanger
Piece of $\frac{1}{4}$-inch thick foam plastic, 18$\frac{1}{2}$ inches by 6$\frac{1}{2}$ inches
Strip of printed cotton 21$\frac{1}{2}$ inches by 7$\frac{1}{2}$ inches
Ribbon for trimming
Matching binding or strip of fabric

Making up
Fold foam plastic round hanger, snipping at centre to go over hook. Stitch edges together. Wrap and secure binding or matching fabric round the hook to cover. Fold over raw edges of fabric strip and press. Slip over hanger. Oversew ends together. Work small running stitches along the base, gathering slightly and back stitching at intervals. Neaten raw edges round hook. Decorate with bow.

4-7

Dressing table set
Box for combs and hairpins

Materials
Base of date box
Soft pencil
$\frac{1}{4}$ yard 36-inch wide flowered cotton fabric
Clear adhesive

Making up
Place fabric right side down on a working surface, put the date box base on it and, holding firmly, lightly trace shape of box onto fabric. Cut two pieces of fabric to this shape.
Place even dots of adhesive down one long side of inside of date box and, wrong side to the base, stick one fabric shape down, so sides project just a fraction up the sides of the box, gluing as you go. Cut a 20$\frac{1}{2}$ inch by 2$\frac{1}{2}$ inch strip of fabric. Press a $\frac{1}{4}$-inch hem along one long side. Stick this down and continue so strip is firmly stuck at lower edge all round inside of box.
Pull fabric up sides and down over the outside of box, and stick down underneath,

sticking second fabric base shape over base of box, to conceal the raw edges of the side piece.

Covered tissue holder

Materials
One small square box tissues
12 inch by 22 inch piece of cotton fabric
Matching thread
One press-stud

Making up
Make a $\frac{1}{4}$-inch hem all round fabric, lay on table wrong side up, and place the box of tissues in the centre. Pull up the longer sides of the fabric and arrange them so they overlap across the top and down the sides of the tissue box.
Holding the box and fabric firmly with one hand, tuck the surplus fabric up at one side as though wrapping a parcel (see illustration), and secure with a few stitches in matching thread. Repeat on other side of box, but stitch a press-stud to fasten the point of fabric that overlaps.

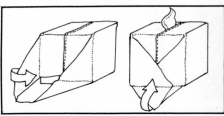

Dressing table tray

Materials
Piece of flowered cotton fabric 14 inches by 9$\frac{1}{4}$ inches or sufficient to fit picture frame
14$\frac{3}{4}$ inches by 10 inches picture frame with backing
Clear adhesive

Making up
Carefully stick the fabric to the frame backing, using clear adhesive. Place the frame on top, fastening into position. If you wish you can cover the fabric with a sheet of glass before fastening down the frame.

Flowered roller bag

Materials
$\frac{1}{2}$ yard 36-inch wide flowered cotton fabric
1 yard $\frac{1}{2}$-inch wide ribbon
Matching thread

Making up
Cut a strip of fabric 25 inches by 14 inches and two circles, each 8$\frac{1}{2}$ inches in diameter. Place circles wrong sides together, stitch together all round: this forms the base. Turn over and press $\frac{1}{4}$-inch hem along one side of fabric strip, turn over another 2 inches and stitch to form channel for ribbon.
Stitch side seam of bag, leaving 2 inch opening at top on inside for ribbon. With right sides together, stitch lower edge of bag to base. Thread ribbon through opening and draw up mouth of bag to close.

8~10

*Tablemat with pocket
and matching tea
and coffee cosies*

Tablemat with pocket

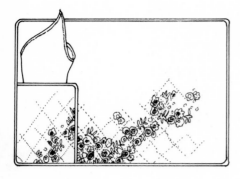

Materials

For each mat:
⅓ yard 36-inch wide quilted cotton
⅓ yard 36-inch wide cotton lining
2 yards piping cord
2 yards cotton bias binding

Making up

Cut out mat and lining to required size (finished size of mat illustrated is 14½ inches by 9½ inches).
Cut out pocket piece about 6 inches by 5½ inches. Allow ½-inch turnings throughout. Cut sufficient piping cord to edge top and side of pocket. Cover piping cord with binding. Pipe this part of pocket (see diagram 1).

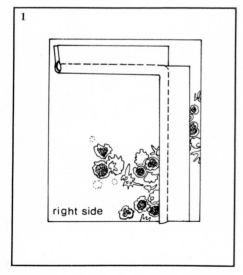

Turn in top allowance and catch down on wrong side. Turn in side allowance and stitch side of pocket to mat.
Measure the outer edge of mat. Cut cord and bias to this length, cover cord and pipe edge of mat.
With right sides together, join lining to mat, sandwiching cord in between and sewing close to piping. Leave one end open for turning. Trim edges and corners.
Turn to right side, turn in ends and slip stitch together.

Tea cosy

Materials

½ yard 36-inch wide quilted cotton
½ yard 36-inch wide cotton lining
1 yard cotton wadding for interlining
2 yards cotton bias binding
2 yards medium thickness piping cord

Making up

The finished size of the cosy illustrated is 12 inches by 9 inches.
Cut out two pieces of fabric for front and back, each 10 inches by 13 inches and one strip, 33 inches by 3¼ inches. ½-inch turnings are allowed throughout. Cut piping cord into two 33 inch lengths and cover with bias binding.
On right side pipe round the sides and top of cosy, on both front and back, nicking binding at corners to get a good right angle (diagram 1).

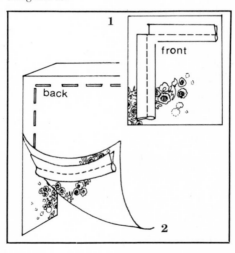

With right sides together, join centre strip to front on three sides, sewing close up to the piping (diagram 2). Join to back in the same way. Turn up all round at hem and herringbone.
Make up lining in same way, omitting piping and pad with cotton wadding, used double.
Make rouleau for the top knot, using scrap of piping cord covered with binding.

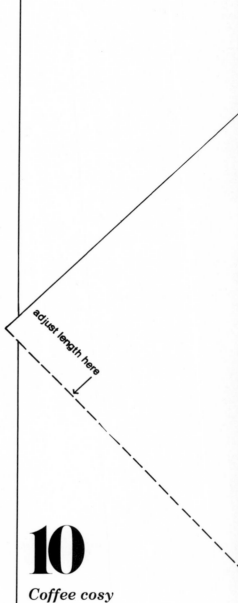

adjust length here

Coffee cosy

Materials

⅝ yard 36-inch wide quilted cotton fabric
⅝ yard 36-inch wide cotton lining
1¼ yards cotton wadding
1¾ yards cotton bias binding
1¾ yards medium thickness piping cord

Making up

Make paper pattern from diagram. Cut out four quarters, adding ½-inch all round for seams. Pipe round two quarters as for tea cosy.
Join the four quarters together, alternating the plain and piped quarters. Make a rouleau loop at top and insert, for top knot. Finish as for tea cosy.

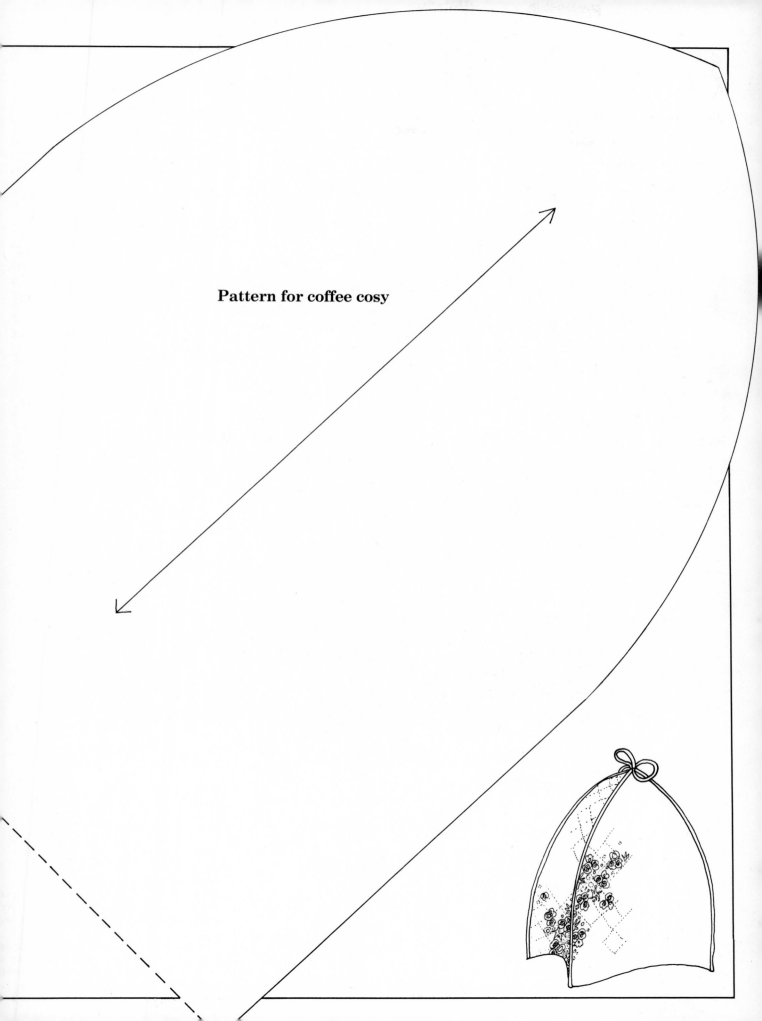

Pattern for coffee cosy

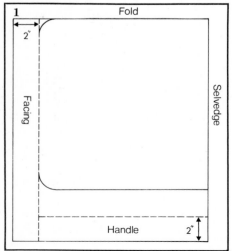

1

Fold

2″

Facing

Selvedge

Handle

2″

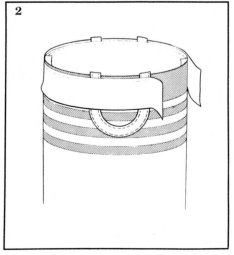

2

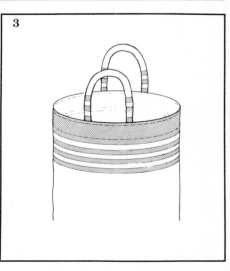

3

11

Canvas shopping bag, lined with polythene

Materials

1¼ yards 18-inch wide deck chair canvas (alternatively use hessian or furnishing fabric)

Strip of polythene about 36 inches by 18 inches

(Finished size of bag is about 15½ inches by 15½ inches)

Making up

Cut a 2 inch wide strip from the selvedge edge of length of canvas. This forms the facing for the top of the bag. Cut two 2 inch strips from the width of the canvas. These are for the handles (diagram 1).

Cut two pieces about 15½ inches square plus ½-inch all round for turnings. Round off the bottom corners (diagram 1).

Place the right sides of bag together with a layer of polythene on top and underneath and pin in position. Sew round sides and bottom of bag through all four layers. Stitch all round bag again, this time stitching the polythene only. This will enclose the raw edges of the bag. Trim off surplus polythene, turn bag to right side.

Make ½-inch wide handles by folding strips in half and then turning in raw edges. Top stitch on either side of handle. These can be lined with polythene if desired.

Position handles at top of bag, on right sides, and pointing down. Place facing round top of bag over handles and stitch (diagram 2). Turn facing to inside and top stitch at top and bottom (diagram 3). When pressing do not use too hot an iron or polythene will melt.

12

Braid and rick-rack trimmings for a plain apron

Materials

Readymade plain apron
Embroidered and rick-rack braids

Making up

Stitch six layers of braid round the hem of the apron and three layers all round the bib, alternating the bands with rick-rack braid. Plain blouses and dresses could also be made special in this way.

13 14

13 *Enchanting bonnets finished with oddments of lace, braid, ribbons and broderie anglaise for a special old-fashioned charm*

14 *These pretty indoor slippers can be made to match a dressing gown and adapted to fit any size of foot*

13

Children's bonnets trimmed with lace and ribbon

Materials

$\frac{3}{8}$ yard 36 inch wide fabric
Oddments of braid, lace, ribbons,
  broderie anglaise

Making up

Make paper patterns from diagram. Cut out
the two shapes A and B adding $\frac{1}{2}$-inch seam
allowances all round.
Fold B in half, right sides to the outside.
With right sides together tack the long strip
B to the head section A. Try on to check fit,
adjust if necessary and then sew. Press and
turn to right side. Bind base of bonnet. Sew
on ribbon ties, then decorate with braid,
lace and ribbon as shown.

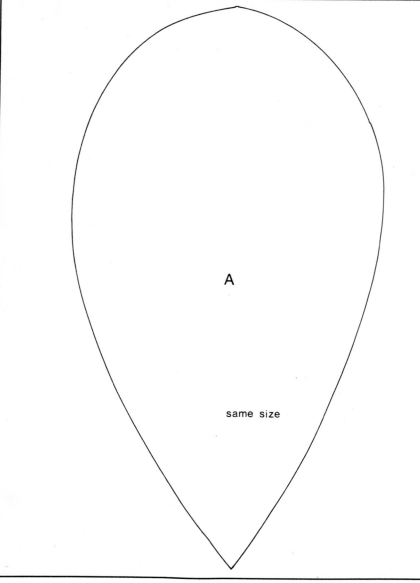

A

same size

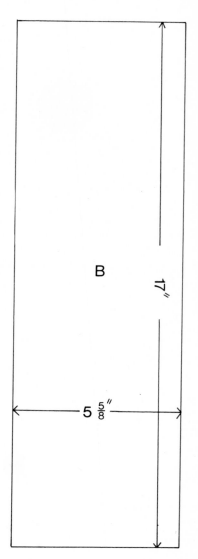

B

17"

5 $\frac{5}{8}$"

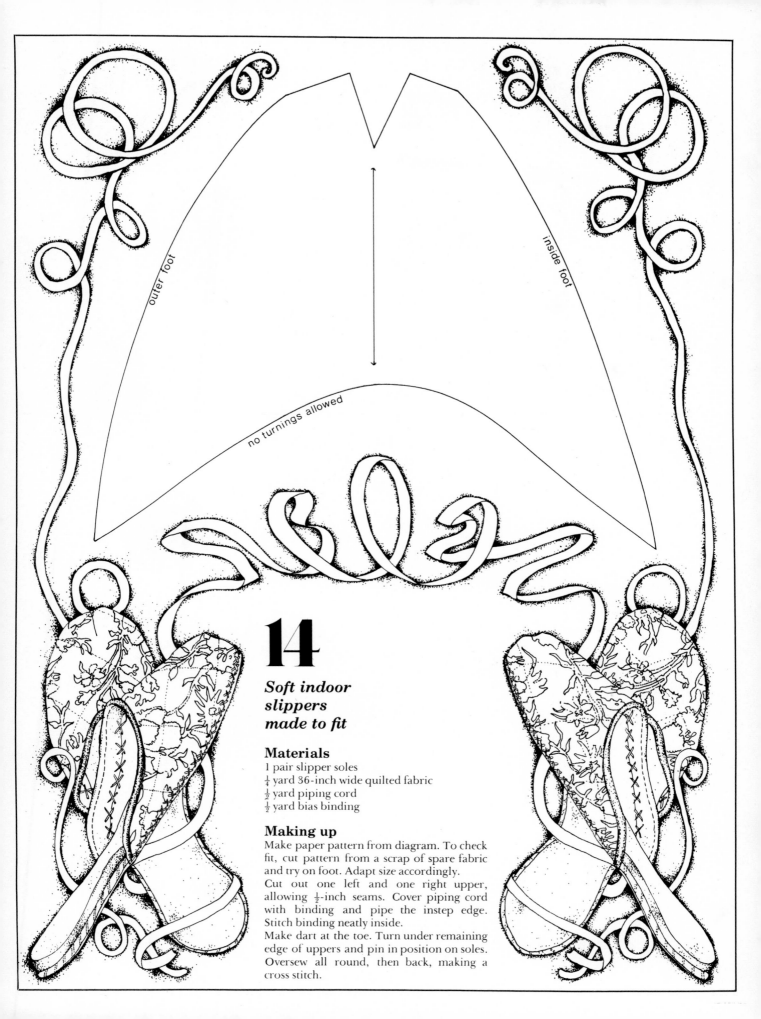

outer foot

inside foot

no turnings allowed

14

Soft indoor slippers made to fit

Materials
1 pair slipper soles
$\frac{1}{4}$ yard 36-inch wide quilted fabric
$\frac{1}{2}$ yard piping cord
$\frac{1}{2}$ yard bias binding

Making up
Make paper pattern from diagram. To check fit, cut pattern from a scrap of spare fabric and try on foot. Adapt size accordingly.
Cut out one left and one right upper, allowing $\frac{1}{2}$-inch seams. Cover piping cord with binding and pipe the instep edge. Stitch binding neatly inside.
Make dart at the toe. Turn under remaining edge of uppers and pin in position on soles. Oversew all round, then back, making a cross stitch.

15 16

Practical apron for a child, cut in one piece with piping around the edges and fastened by press studs on the shoulders

Brightly coloured felt shoe bags to keep shoes clean and protected, whether hung in a wardrobe or packed in a suitcase

15

Child's apron

Materials
1½ yards 36-inch wide cotton
Two press studs
4 yards bias binding
(To fit a 20 inch chest)

Making up
Make paper pattern from diagram. Place to fold of fabric and cut out. Open out pieces and place wrong sides together so that apron is made up double. Tack together and bind right round edges with bias binding. Stitch on press studs where indicated to fasten.

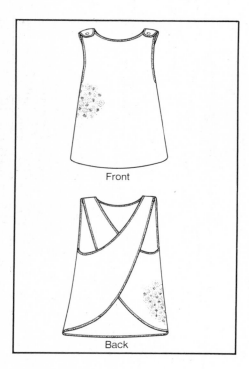

Front

Back

16

Felt shoebags

Materials
Two strips felt, each about 16 inches
   by 9½ inches
About 1 yard upholsterer's binding
1 yard matching cord

Making up
Place the two pieces of felt together. Fold the binding in half. Sandwich it in between the two layers of felt around sides and base with fold facing inwards and stitch in place.
Turn down top of bag for 1 inch and stitch to make channel for cord. Turn to right side. Insert cord in channel and tie the ends together.

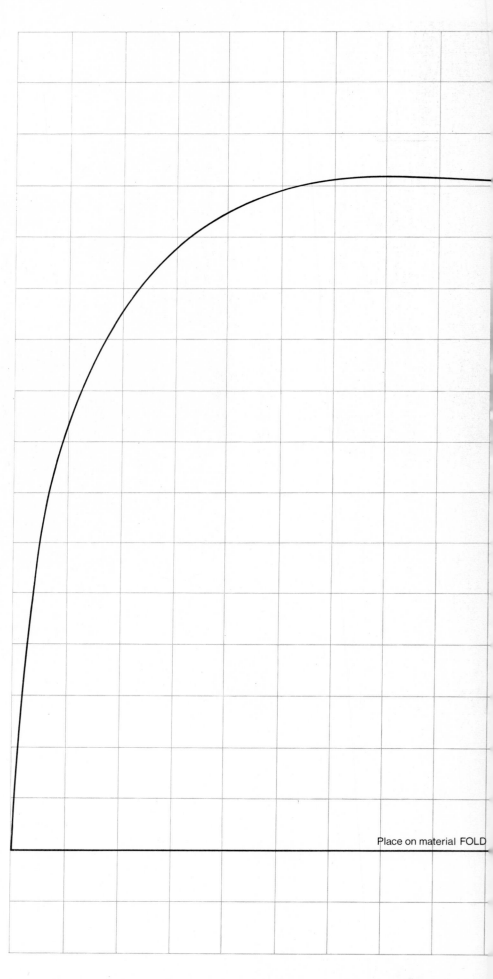

Place on material FOLD

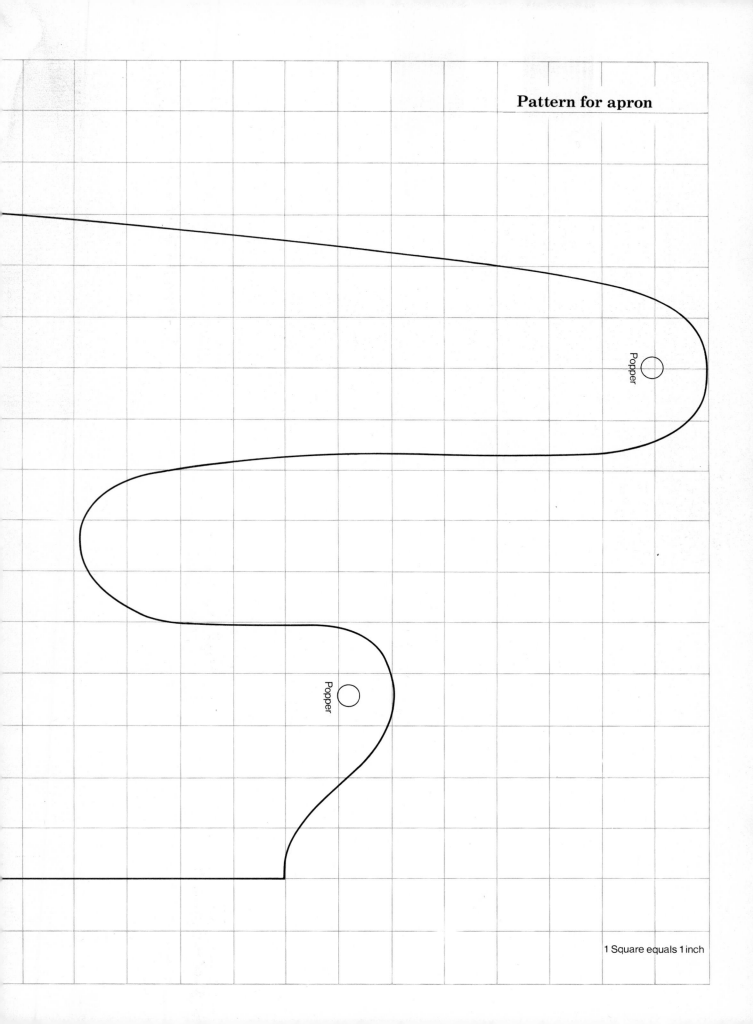

Pattern for apron

Popper

Popper

1 Square equals 1 inch

17-20 21

*Matching desk set.
Paperclip holder,
diary, binder and
blotter, covered in
harmonizing material*

*Wise owl money box
made of papier mâché
round a balloon base
with felt feathers
and big round eyes*

17–20

Paperclip box

Materials
One round wooden box
Scraps of Madras cotton, striped and plain
Clear adhesive

Making up
Place plain cotton flat on a working surface and put the box on top; holding firmly, lightly trace shape of box onto fabric. Cut two pieces of fabric to this shape.
Place even dots of adhesive down one long side of inside of box and, with wrong side to base, stick one fabric shape down, so sides project just a fraction up the sides of the box, gluing as you go.
Measure round inside of box. Cut strip of plain fabric this length by depth of box allowing ¾-inch overlap at top. Cut strip of striped fabric the same length. Press ⅛-inch hem along one long edge of plain strip. Stick this down firmly at lower edge all round box. Pull fabric up sides and down over the outside of box and stick down.
Similarly press narrow hem along long edge of striped fabric strip and stick all around sides of box, tucking raw short edge under to neaten; glue this down. Pull raw edge of striped fabric under box and stick. Finish by neatly gluing second circle of plain fabric to base of box.

Covered diary

Materials
Piece of fabric, 14½ inches by 11 inches
Clear adhesive
Large diary, 8¼ inches by 5 inches
Large sheet of patterned paper

Making up
Place fabric flat on a working surface and centre diary on it. Open diary and turn fabric in on cover for 1½ inches gluing both sides. Repeat with back cover then slit fabric each side of spine and push fabric flaps down inside spine. Then stick remaining sides of fabric cover to inside of diary.
Cut pieces of patterned paper to size of inside of front and back covers, and carefully stick over turned-in fabric to trim.

Covered binder

Materials
One 12½ inch by 10 inch binder
½ yard 36-inch wide striped Madras cotton
⅜ yard 36-inch wide plain cotton
Clear adhesive

Making up
Cut striped cotton into a rectangle, 27½ inches by 13 inches and a strip 13 inches by 2½ inches.
Cut plain cotton into two pieces, each 12½ inches by 10¼ inches. Stick the large piece of Madras cotton to the binder in the same way as for the diary. Turn the two pieces of plain cotton under so they fit the inside back and inside front covers of binder, leaving ¼-inch all round, and stick down. Turn raw edges of Madras cotton strip under and stick down inside spine of binder.

Blotting pad

Materials
Piece of thick cardboard, 18 inches by 11½ inches
¼ yard 36-inch wide cotton fabric
Clear adhesive
Sheet of stiff dark paper, cut to same size as cardboard

Making up
Cut four squares of fabric, each 7½ inches by 5 inches. Fold one across triangularly and place across one corner of board, as shown in picture. Mitre fabric at back of board and stick down. Repeat with other three fabric squares and stick a sheet of stiff paper neatly down over the back to hide the raw edges.

21

Wise owl moneybox

Materials
Balloon
Vaseline
Newspaper strips
Wallpaper paste
Brush
Coloured felts
Scissors
Fabric glue
Dried peas

Making up
Decide on the size of your money box, and blow up a balloon accordingly, tying a knot at the top. Grease the balloon lightly with vaseline all over and then apply about six layers of newspaper strips, with a layer of wallpaper paste between each. Leave each layer near a radiator overnight to become thoroughly dry before applying the next layer.
After the sixth layer has dried, burst the balloon and take it out. Then tidy up the hole it has left and cut it into a slot large enough to take money and also to shake it out again.
Pour some dried peas inside the papier mâché shape to act as a weight, so that it will stand upright when you are sticking on the 'feathers'.
Draw the owl onto the papier mâché (diagram 1). Decide which colour felt you wish to use for your background then cut out and glue a piece onto the chest. Decide on another colour to use for the 'feathers'. Cut out a rectangle of this and cover the money slit as if you are making a covered buttonhole (diagram 2).

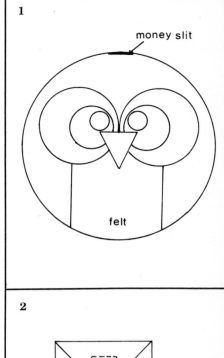

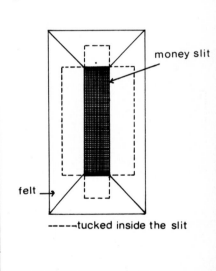

Cut out the feathers (see diagram 3) in felt. Starting from the outside edge of the chest and working from the bottom up, begin to stick on the 'feathers' (diagram 4). Apply the glue only to the top edge of the 'feather' and overlap each layer slightly.
Continue round the eyes, front and over the top until the owl is covered, including the money slit—which can easily be found by parting the 'feathers'.
To make the ears, stitch two feather shapes together and glue in place so that they stand upright (diagram 5).
For the owl's chest glue the feathers in exactly the same way as the back, but grade the colours to make them more interesting. At the edge where the chest and body 'feathers' meet, make the body 'feathers' overlap the chest.
For the eyes, cut two large oval shapes in orange felt, then two smaller yellow ones. Cut two small white circles and finally two smaller black ones. Position them on the yellow and orange surrounds for the best expression, before sticking them down.
Cut a triangle for the beak, and glue in place.

3

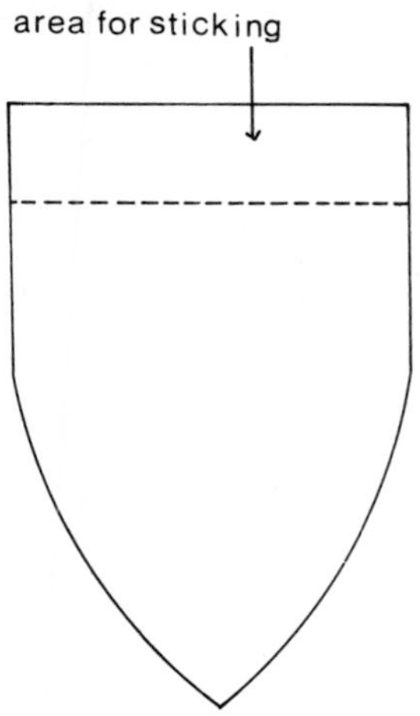

area for sticking

4

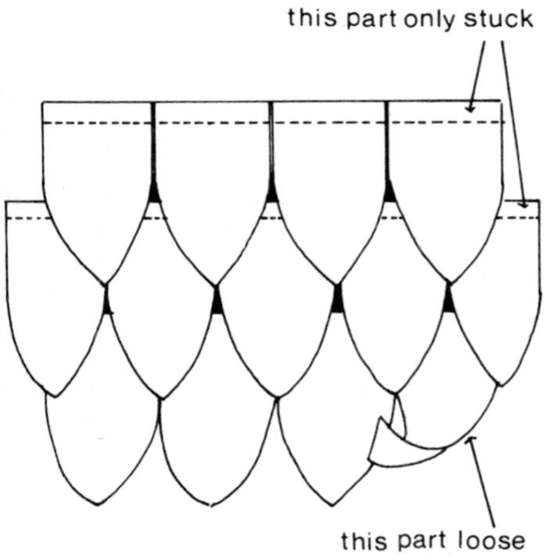

this part only stuck

this part loose

5

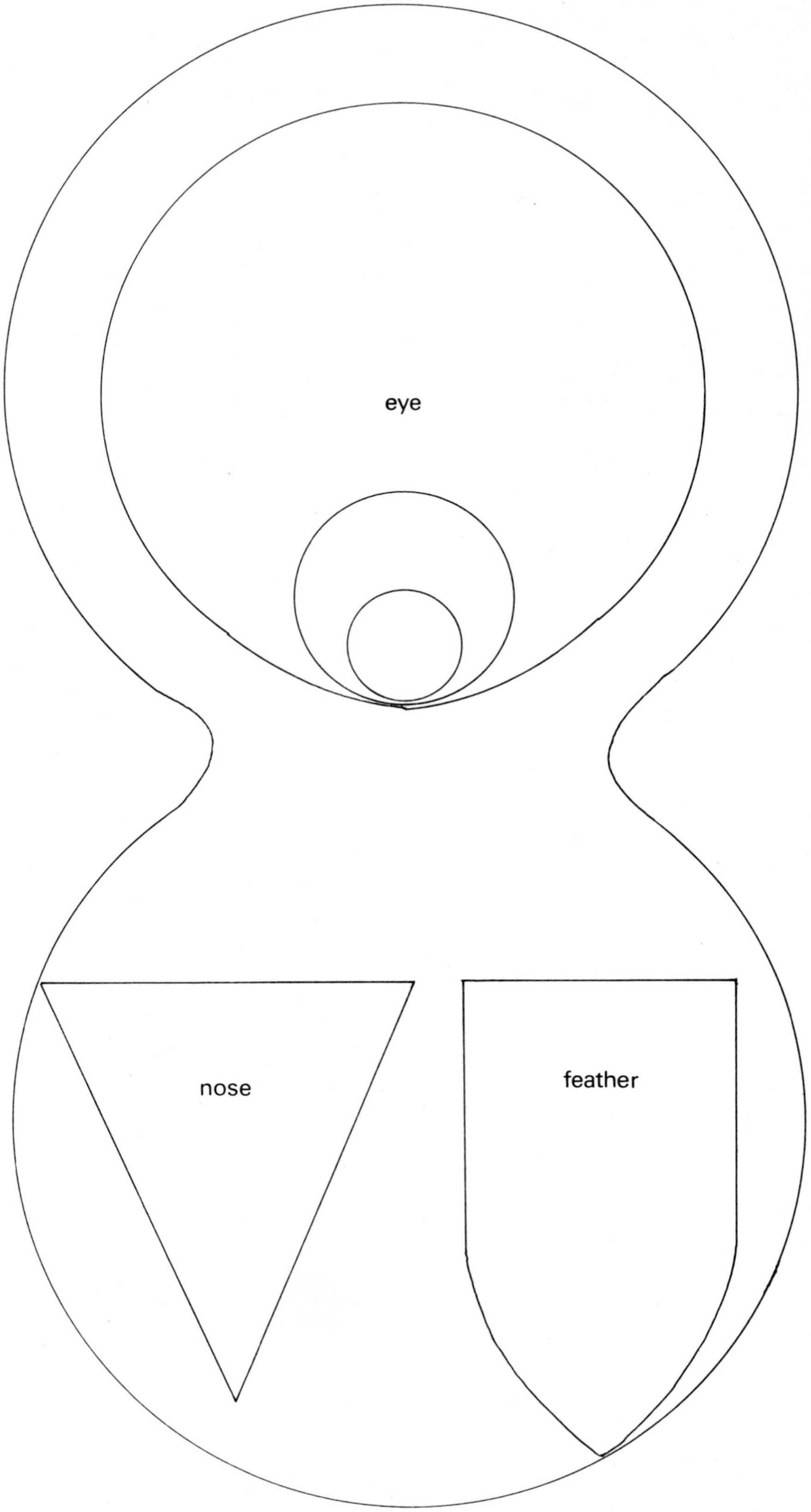

eye

nose

feather

Trace shapes for an owl 9½—12 inches tall

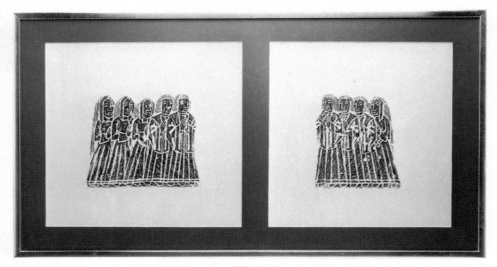

22

Brass rubbings to make into pictures or wall-hangings

Materials

Lining paper
Masking tape
Heelball (available from most art shops or shoe repairers)
Scissors
Clean cloth

Making up

Clean brass with cloth to remove grit. Place paper over brass and hold it in position with strips of masking tape. Using finger and clean cloth press around the edge of the rubbing to make an outline to work inside.

Begin rubbing with the heelball starting at the top and working down to the bottom. Press hard with the heelball for a dark even effect—holding the paper down firmly with your other hand.

When the rubbing is completed, brush away any loose bits of heelball and polish with a clean cloth to make the wax shine.

This technique can be applied to manhole covers, wrought iron, horse brasses or leaves (glue these on a piece of card before rubbing). If you choose to make a rubbing from a brass in a church, remember that permission should be obtained in advance—some churches do not allow rubbing on Sundays, and a fee is usually charged.

To mount the rubbing, either frame it as a picture, or hang it by taking two pieces of rod a little wider than the paper. Roll one end of the paper round a rod and glue. Do the same with the other end. Knot a hanging cord to both ends of the top rod and hang.

Manhole covers make decorative rubbings

23-25

Three bolster cushions, ribbon trimmed, printed and neatly piped

Materials

Basic bolster foundation:
$\frac{1}{2}$ yard down-proof cambric or ticking
Feathers for filling
Lace bolster:
$\frac{1}{2}$ yard 36-inch wide lace
$\frac{1}{2}$ yard 36-inch wide satin
About 6 yards each of baby ribbon in two different colours
Piped bolster:
$\frac{3}{4}$ yard 36-inch wide silk or tussore
1 yard piping cord
Two $1\frac{1}{2}$-inch diameter buttons covered in matching fabric
Printed bolster:
$\frac{5}{8}$ yard 36-inch wide cotton
Two 1-inch diameter brass curtain rings

Making up

Bolster foundation: Cut out a rectangle about 18 inches wide and required length of bolster. With right sides together stitch long side and ends, leaving opening for turning. Fill well with feathers. Oversew opening firmly. Fold in corners to form rounded ends and stitch.

Lace bolster: Make a satin bolster cover in same way as foundation, gathering ends to fit. Make a tight cover of lace to go over this, turn in ends and again draw up with gathering threads.

Make a knot of looped ribbons for each end (see diagram) and sew into gathered ends of lace cover (use the ribbon double and fan out afterwards).

Printed bolster: Using full width fabric make a tight cover for bolster in same way as foundation, leaving ends open. Slip onto the bolster. Fold open ends inside the cover and then draw through curtain rings, pulling up tight to bolster and fanning out like a cracker.

Piped bolster: Cut rectangle of fabric about 14 inches by 18 inches and two 4 inch by 36 inch strips. Make a slip cover slightly shorter than the foundation, leaving ends open.

Cut two lengths of piping cord, the circumference of bolster and two $1\frac{1}{2}$-inch wide bias strips to cover piping. Pipe each open end of cover. Gather up long strip to fit each end and with right sides together stitch to cover, sandwiching piping in between and stitching close to cord. Turn to right side.

Turn in raw edges and gather up the open ends as tightly as possible. Finish with covered button at each end.

26

Tin mugs decorated with transfers

Materials
Soak-on transfers
Mugs or plates
Scissors
Tissues
Clear polyurethane varnish (optional)

Making up
Clean the surface of the plate or mug thoroughly, making sure that it is quite dry and free from grease.

Cut out each transfer separately and soak each one for about a minute in warm water. Place it in position and, while holding the white non-transfer paper between finger and thumb, very gently slide the picture onto the surface. As the transfer is still movable until it dries out, you can adjust the transfer as you wish. Blot off the surplus water with a tissue.

If you wish to make the transfers completely waterproof, wait until they are thoroughly dry and then paint over the picture with a thin coat of clear polyurethane varnish—but remember that utensils treated in this way are for decoration only. You should not eat or drink from a polyurethane varnished surface.

27

Gay paper collage for a child's room

Materials
Card or thick paper
Scissors
Cow gum
Cutouts
Plain acetate

Making up
Stiff white card or cartridge paper are best for the background, cut to whatever size you wish.

Then start collecting scraps—Christmas and birthday cards, stickers, wrapping and tissue paper, cereal packets, travel brochures, comics, snippets of pretty non-fraying fabrics, wallpaper.

Begin by cutting everything out—even if you find you have more pieces than you need. Cut round the edge of each shape so that the pieces can be overlapped.

Assemble the collage first, without sticking the cutouts down, to make an exciting design. When you have decided on the final arrangement, begin sticking, starting from the left and working across.

Cover the collage with plain, clear acetate, fixing it with sticky tape at the back to keep the collage clean and protected.

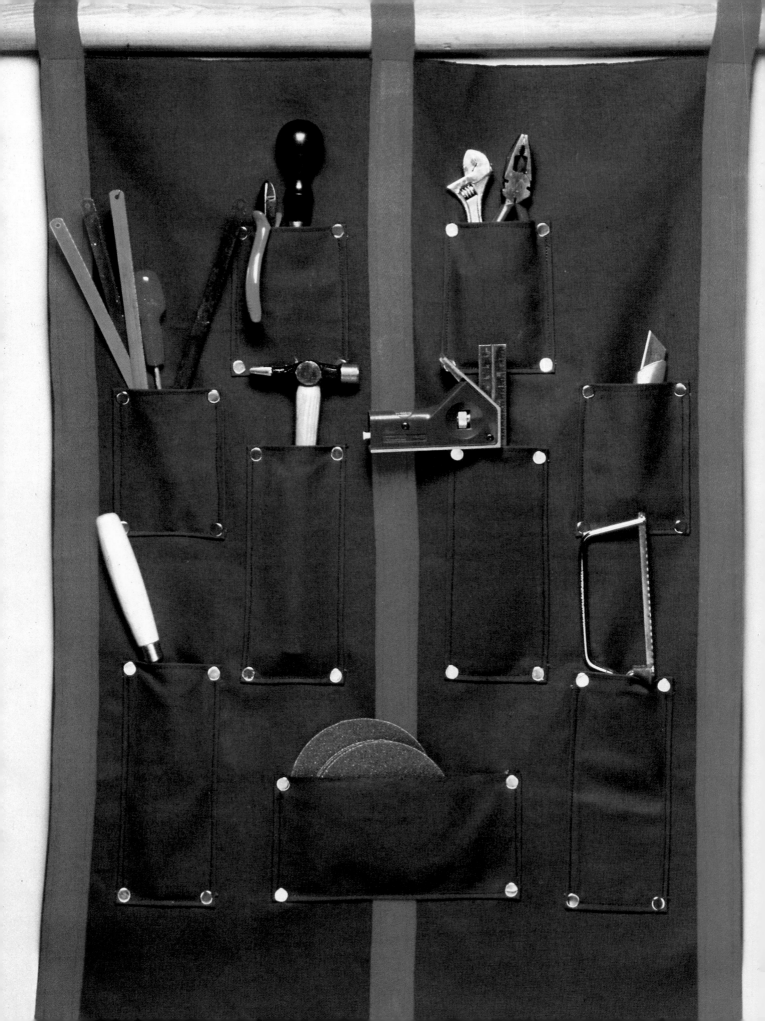

28

Tough and practical tool tidy

Materials
1 yard of 36 inch wide canvas
3½ yards webbing, 1½ inches wide in
   contrasting colour
36 decorative studs
Thread to match canvas
Needles
Pins
Scissors

Making up back
Cut 26 inch length from fabric. Reserve remaining 10 inch piece for making the pockets (called piece B later on).
Cut webbing into 42 inch lengths, put aside.
Turn under raw edges and pin webbing to wrong side (raw edge side), turning under ½ inch at bottom. At top, loop tape over back, turn under raw end and pin in place. Make sure that the loops are even across top. Stitch in place with two rows of stitching. Stitch third length of tape down the centre doing the top and bottom ends the same as the sides.

Making up pockets
Take fabric piece B and divide into two 18 inch lengths (diagram 1). Divide one piece into 4 equal widths (diagram 2). From remaining 18 inch piece, cut a piece 5 inches wide (diagram 3). Fold remaining 13 inches in half and cut; fold these in half and cut (diagram 4) so that you have four small pockets.
Turn under raw edges and baste. Position on backing, determining where the heaviest or largest objects will be to distribute weight evenly, and stitch in place.
Hammer studs into corners of pockets.

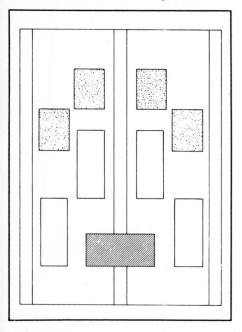

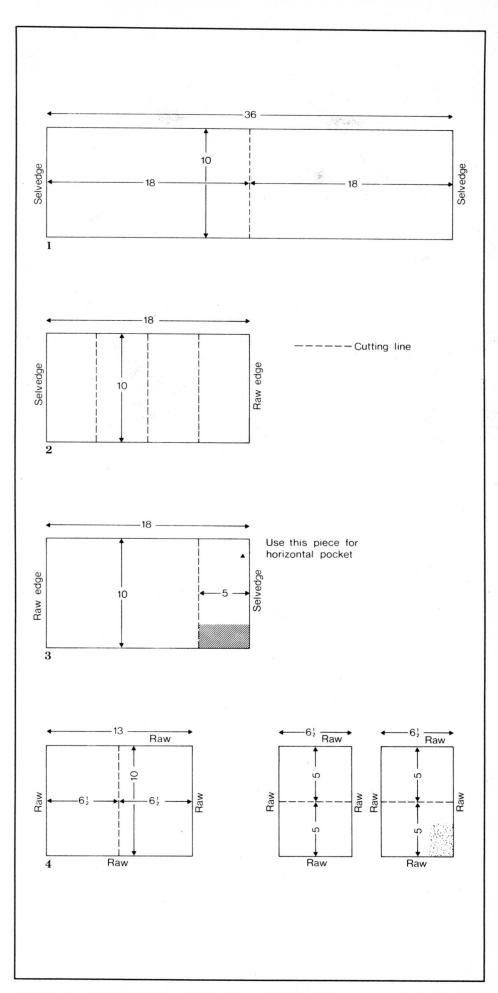

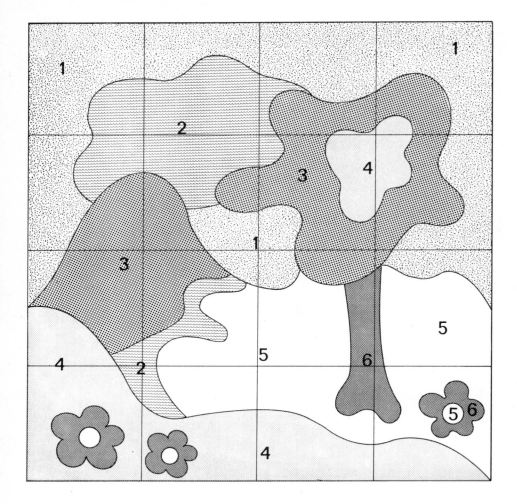

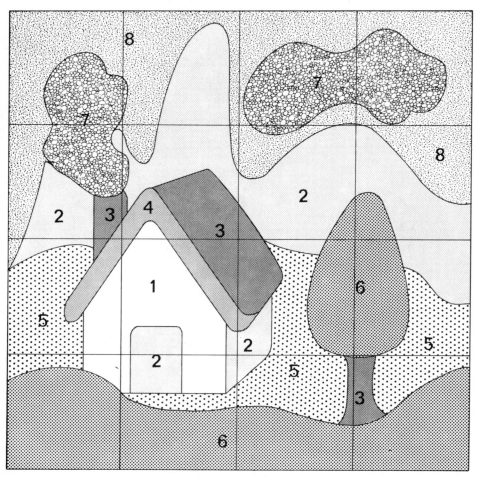

Six cushions in matching colours to embroider for a rich mass of colour

Materials

Fabric:

Single canvas, 16 threads to the inch. 24 inches by 24 inches for each cushion. Dress wool or cotton repp, 22 inches by 22 inches for backing.

Cushion pad.

Yarn: Anchor Tapisserie Wool. The number of skeins required is shown in brackets after each colour number.

(Finished measurement: about 20 inches by 20 inches.)

Making up

Each cushion is worked in the same way. On a large sheet of paper, divide a twenty inch square into a five inch grid. Enlarge the design, matching the lines in each small square to the large. Outline the finished drawing with a felt tipped pen. On a flat surface, fix the canvas over the drawing and transfer the design lines and the twenty inch square outline.

Work the embroidery in rows of brick stitch, making small stitches to fill in at the design lines. Stitch with a loose tension.

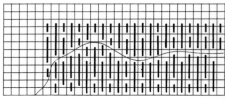

To make up cushion: With drawing pins, block the finished canvas face up onto a board covered with damp blotting paper. Leave for twenty-four hours to dry. Machine stitch backing and canvas right sides together —leaving one side open. Trim seam. Turn to right side and insert cushion pad. Oversew the remaining seam.

29

Tree Design. 1.0497 (9) Light grey; **2.**0105 (7) Light violet; **3.**0246 (9) Dark green; **4.**0265 (9) Light green; **5.**0306 (9) Yellow; **6.**019 (3) Red

30

House Design. 1.0295 (4) Yellow; **2.**0314 (12) Orange; **3.**019 (5) Red; **4.**063 (2) Pink; **5.**0265 (9) Light green; **6.**0246 (9) Dark green; **7.**0185 (5) Turquoise; **8.**0399 (9) Dark grey

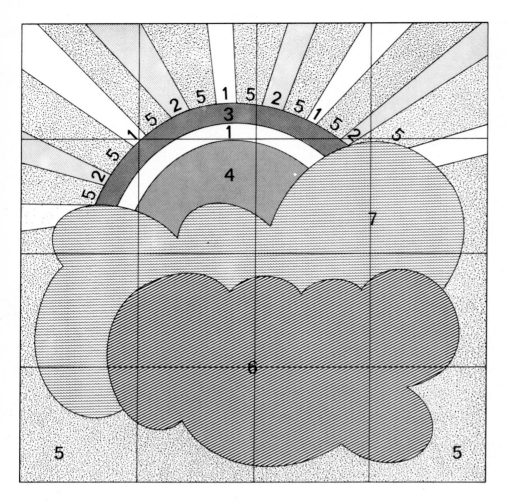

31

Sun Design. **1.**0295 (4) Yellow; **2.**0314 (4) Orange; **3.**019 (3) Red; **4.**063 (3) Pink; **5.**0497 (15) Light grey; **6.**0105 (9) Light violet; **7.**0872 (9) Dull lilac

32

Moon and Stars Design. **1.**0497 (2) Light grey; **2.**0295 (9) Yellow; **3.**0105 (15) Light violet; **4.**0107 (21) Dark violet

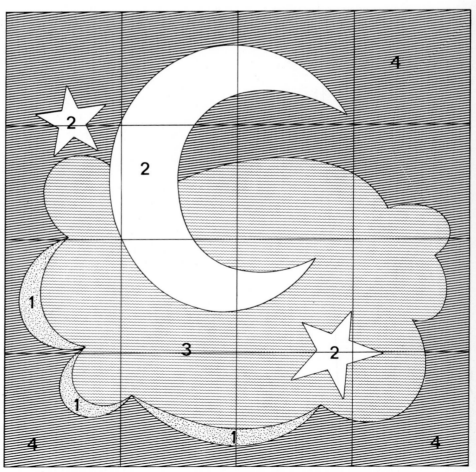

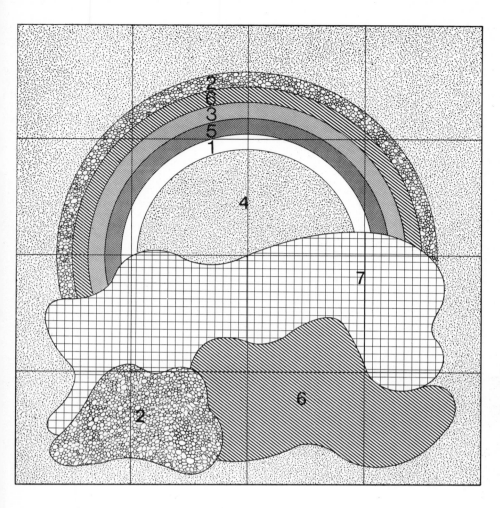

33

Rainbow Design. **1.**0306 (1) Yellow; **2.**0185 (4) Turquoise; **3.**063 (2) Pink; **4.**0497 (24) Light grey; **5.**019 (1) Red; **6.**0107 (7) Dark violet; **7.**0399 (9) Dark grey

34

Thunder and Lightning. **1.**063 (4) Pink; **2.**0107 (12) Dark violet; **3.**0185 (12) Turquoise; **4.**0105 (21) Light violet
Needle: Tapestry No. 18
Stitch: Brick

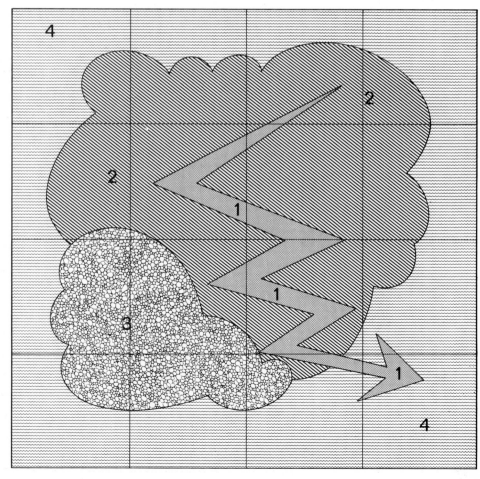

35 36

Big bold lion rug made in four separate sections. The individual sections can be used for cushions or wall-hangings

Plaited wool rug as fresh and bright as a bouquet of flowers. The wool is used double thickness for extra strength and durability

35

Bold lion design for a rug, cushion or wall-hanging

Using cut wool with a latchet hook is one of the easiest and fastest ways of making a rug. The straightforward technique produces a warm, hard-wearing, thick pile that will last for a lifetime. There are three ways you can set about making a pile rug. You can buy a kit with the design already printed onto the canvas, with the correct amounts of wool in each colour included: you can buy plain canvas with a charted design and you choose your own colour scheme, or, if you are adventurous, you can just buy a strip of canvas and make up a design of your own.

Materials

Canvas: this comes in various widths from 12-inch to 48-inch, so there is plenty of choice for whatever size of rug you make. The rug illustrated is four 24-inch squares. The canvas you need is 10 holes to 3-inch rug canvas and is usually divided up with either red or brown threads making squares, 3 inches by 3 inches, ten holes by ten holes.

Wool: the correct wool for hooked rugs is a coarse 6 ply rug wool. This is available either in skeins, which can be cut to whatever length you want by winding the wool round a grooved wooden gauge and then slicing along the groove with a sharp razor blade, or you can buy it pre-cut in bundles of 320 pieces. These are called units and one unit will cover 3 squares. For the over-sewn edge, buy skeins of wool to match.

Tools: a latchet-hook is the only tool you will need and it is available from any handicraft shop. Shaped like a large crochet hook with a wooden handle, it has a hinged latched which closes the open end of the hook as you make the rug knot, and prevents the canvas from becoming entangled.

Making up

Lay your canvas on a table with the full length stretching away from you. A good plan is to secure it with a heavy weight or a pile of books at the other end. Then, to prevent the cut ends from fraying, fold the end of the canvas over for about 2 inches (frayed edge uppermost) exactly matching each hole with the hole beneath. It makes the rug easier to work if you tack this in position. Now work the first few rows of knots through this double thickness, so losing the rough ends in the pile of the rug.

To make a really hard-wearing rug, finish it with an oversewing stitch round the edges. Leave the outside thread of canvas free and one square at either side next to the selvedge so that they can be oversewn at the end. Start working the rug from left to right (right to left if you are left handed), and keep working in parallel rows. Don't

be tempted to do patches of the pattern and then join them up as this will give a very uneven finished appearance and also, with the thick wool, it is easy to miss squares.

To work: Make each of the individual squares following the diagram. Each little square stands for one knot and two strands are always used for each knot. For the rug you will need four squares, with the lion reversed on two of them so that the lion's heads point inwards. Single squares can also be used for cushions or wall-hangings.

To estimate amounts you need:

Work out the number of holes in each coloured section of the design. The resulting number divided by 320 will give you the number of wool units you need in each colour.

The 4 movement knot

1. Fold a cut length of wool in half and, holding it between the thumb and index finger of the left hand, loop it around the neck of the latchet-hook.
2. Still holding onto the ends of the wool, insert the hook under the first of the horizontal (weft) threads.
3. Turning the hook a little to the right, take the ends of the wool around the hook.
4. Pull the latchet-hook under the weft thread and through the loop of wool, catching the two ends in the hook as the latchet closes automatically.
5. Pull the ends of the wool tight to check that the knot is firm. The tuft will finish up lying towards you.

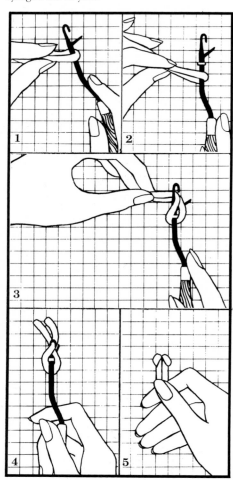

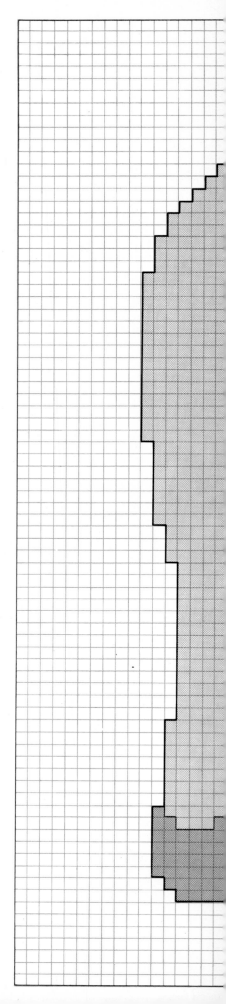

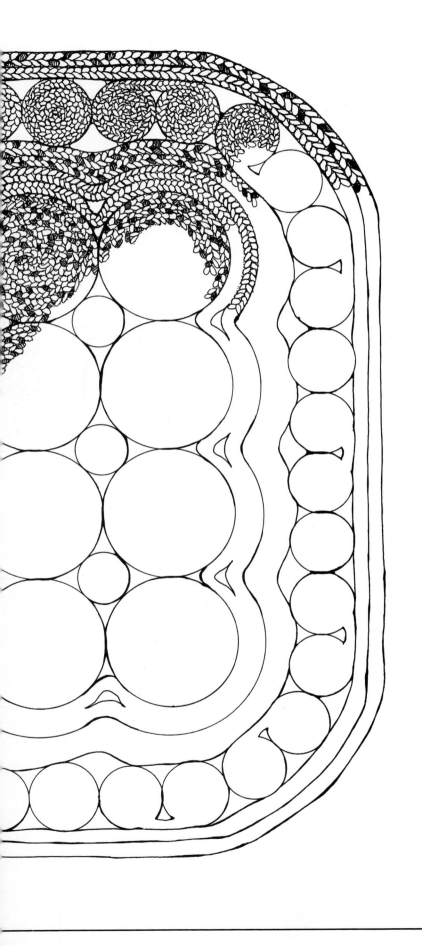

36

Plaited wool rug in bright colours

Materials

The following 50 gr. balls of Pingouin rug wool:

six balls 152 capucine
five balls 102 tilleul
five balls 101 mousse
three balls 151 azalée
three balls 155 turquoise
three balls 161 jonquille
three balls 103 bouton d'or
two balls 143 rouge clair
two balls 127 bleu mer
two balls 105 edelweiss
two balls 142 quetsche
two balls 134 bleu franc
one ball 109 muflier
one ball 128 delft
one ball 136 marine

As bright as a flower bed, this rug consists of plaits of wool woven in and out of one another. The secret of its strength lies in the fact that you use the wool double.

Making up

To make the plaits, cut threads of wool to different lengths, between $23\frac{1}{2}$ inches and 47 inches. Plait them together using the strands double (see illustration) weave these threads together mingling the various colours.

To make the circles coil up the plaits and stitch them on the reverse side. Make the circles in two sizes, 24 large ones with a 7 inch diameter and 15 smaller ones with a 3 inch diameter. Lay out the coloured circles in the shape of the rug, as shown, then stitch them together.

Next sew two red braids around the outside edge, followed by two multi-coloured braids. Make red circles $4\frac{1}{4}$ inches in diameter, then double circles of lime and moss green, $3\frac{1}{2}$ inches in diameter. Stitch the final braids of lime and red around the outer edge to complete.

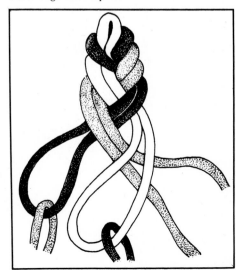

37 38

37 *Rich, elegant evening bag in cool white satin with braid trimming for a luxurious evening accessory*

38 *Unusual paperweight made of plastic, enclosing an exotic assortment of coral and different shells*

39

Horse-brass belts

40

Decorated box

41-46

Jewellery made with shells, beads and pebbles

37

White satin evening bag

Materials

About ½ yard 36-inch wide satin
About ½ yard 36-inch wide lining
About 1¼ yards very fine piping cord
About ¾ yard 3-inch wide furnishing braid
Paper for pattern

Making up

First make a paper pattern. Carefully measure the size of the frame from the holes on the outside.

The frame illustrated is about 7 inches by 2 inches and the finished bag about 9 inches by 8 inches.

Draw pattern out accurately and extend it to the shape and size bag you want, rounding off the lower corners. When making a rectangular shape, cut the bottom slightly wider than the top, otherwise it will give the impression of being narrower. In the same way, if you add strips of braid or decoration, make them fan out towards the bottom and not run parallel.

Cut out your paper pattern and try it on the frame, making any adjustments now. Cut out back and front in satin and lining. Measure round bag from hinge to hinge and cut out gusset strip to this length and not more than ½-inch wide, plus turnings. Allow ½-inch turnings throughout. Cut 1½-inch wide bias strip, twice length of gusset plus top of bag. Cut furnishing braid into two pieces and position on front of bag. Tack the braid into place from the wrong side of fabric. Cut two pieces of piping cord to length of gusset. Cover piping cord with bias strip and pipe round the edge of bag, on the right side of bag, from hinge point to hinge point. Repeat for the back.

With right sides together join gusset strip to the bag front sandwiching in piping and stitching close to cord. Join gusset to back,

in the same way. The piping should be eased away to nothing just before the hinge points.

Cut piping cord to fit frame exactly over holes. Cover cord with bias and pipe across the top front of the bag. Neaten ends of bias and cord.

Make up lining in same way, omitting piping. Turn in hem allowances and, with wrong sides together, slip stitch lining to front of bag. Check that the bag fits the frame exactly or adjust the size before you sew.

Turn in edge of gusset strip at hinge level and slip stitch to lining. At back slip stitch sides of opening only. Sew the top front and sides of bag to the frame with long tacking stitches, working through the holes of frame. Sew on the join line of the piping and stitches will not show, then stitch back, reversing the stitching. Adjust the length of back of the bag, turn in and slip stitch lining in place.

Sew the back of the bag to the frame in the same way as for front. These tacking stitches can be embroidered over with closely worked buttonhole stitch to look like a fine cord, or stitching can be covered with braid.

38

Plastic paperweight

Materials

Glazed mould
Releasing wax
Small tin of liquid plastic
Plastic hardener
Small measuring cup marked in millilitres
Small aluminium dish
Plastic colour pigment
(All these items can be obtained in a 'Plasticraft' kit)
Shells and coral
Scrap of felt
Glue

Making up

Prepare mould, clean with soft cloth. Then wipe round with a small amount of the releasing wax, allow to dry and polish up. Repeat.

Pour 10 ml. of liquid plastic into measuring cup and add five drops of plastic hardener, mix thoroughly for one minute, then pour into mould. Leave to harden.

When hard place item to be encased upside down in mould. Now continue pouring in the liquid plastic and hardener mixture to completely encase item. If you wish to put other things in, as in the paperweight illustrated, pour plastic mixture to half way up coral and allow to harden; then, working in layers, add small shells and fill with more plastic mixture until all are covered.

To make a coloured base mix 10 ml. liquid plastic and colour pigment with 10 drops of hardener, mix thoroughly. When last layer has hardened pour in colour mixture, if not enough make more until satisfied. Allow to harden overnight.

To remove from mould immerse in very hot water for ten minutes, remove and immerse upside down in very cold water, repeat until mould is released. Sand down base until smooth, polish face with soft cloth and finish with a felt base, glued on.

39

Belts made with horsebrasses or old buckles

Materials

Horsebrass or old decorative metal buckles
About 1 yard of velvet ribbon or braid, the diameter of buckle
2 large press studs

Making up

Loop velvet through buckle and sew back on wrong side. Hem free end. Sew press studs behind buckle and to right side of the fabric at other end. If using velvet, try running rows of machine stitching ½ inch apart down the length of the belt to give a padded effect, before making up.

40

Box decorated with paper scraps

Materials

A prettily shaped wooden box in good condition
Scraps to decorate
Paper lace cake strip
Sandpaper
Strong paste or adhesive
Enamel or semi-gloss paint
Clear varnish

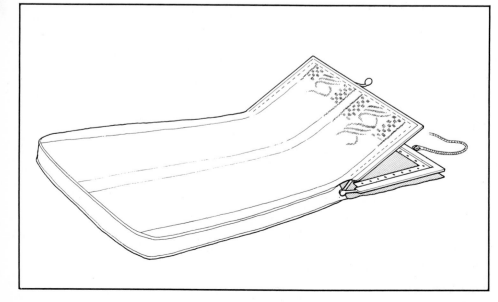

Making up

Sandpaper the box down to get a good smooth surface. Paint or spray it and leave to dry thoroughly. Two coats may be necessary.

Arrange your scraps and stick them down (use a large motif for the centre surrounded by small ones, or use a pretty print or postcard). Cut the beaded edge from the cake paper and stick round top of box to finish. Varnish box. If a lining is necessary use prettily printed paper.

41-46
Shell jewellery

Materials

Cardboard
Epoxy resin adhesive
Beads, shells and pebbles
Raffia
Wine corks
Plaster of Paris
Silver chain
String
Fine wire

Making up

Bottom left: The small wall picture is made by cutting out a picture from a magazine and gluing it to a shallow lid from a carton. The one illustrated is approximately $3\frac{1}{2}$ inches in diameter.

To frame the picture, simply collect pretty stones and shells from the beach and a few beads (usually available from haberdashery departments) and glue them to the picture with epoxy resin adhesive. The picture can then be hung by the rim from a nail in the wall, or alternatively used as a decorative lid to the container.

Centre left: The miniature charm is made by cutting a disc from a cork, and surrounding it with a frame of plaited string. A pendant loop is made with the string or a piece of fine wire.

Glue the string frame firmly to the cork and decorate the inner rim with fine mixed beads and a combination of shells and beads on the frame. Use the central area to glue on the name of the wearer.

Centre top: The circular decoration is made with seven $\frac{1}{8}$-inch thick discs cut from ordinary wine corks, glued together with epoxy resin adhesive. A picture cut from a magazine, or a photograph, is glued to the centre disc and cutouts, beads and shells are glued to the remaining discs.

Centre bottom: For the pendant, beautiful blue-grey mussel shells are hung on a band of thin plaited raffia by drilling a small hole

in the top of the shell.

To make the fastener, tie a loop in one end of the raffia, and attach a cork disc to the other end of the raffia. Decorate the cork with small shells and beads glued with epoxy resin adhesive. The disc is then passed through the loop to form the fastening.

Centre right: Another pendant on a thin silver chain (available from most jewellery stores). The photograph is simply glued to a piece of cardboard and the enchanting frame is made from rows of tiny blue and green beads with five small everlasting flowers glued at the top. The chain can be passed through the cardboard at the top where the hole is concealed by the flowers.

Far right: Crab claw necklace. Boil the pincers to make them quite clean, and fill with liquid plaster. While the plaster is still wet make a little loop with fine wire and insert one end into the plaster to set firmly. A plaited raffia chain can then be passed through the loop.

47
Enamelled shells

Materials

Enamel paint
Brushes
Shells or tins to decorate
Polyurethane varnish

Making up

To make pretty soap dishes or ashtrays from scallop shells, wash the shells very thoroughly before you begin. When the shell is dry, enamel the surface, allow to dry and finish with a coat of varnish.

To decorate boxes and tins (coffee tins, film cassette tins and so on) apply the enamel, and add transfers as described in No. 26. These make delightful storage jars or pill boxes.

48

*Linen purse
embroidered in
cross stitch*

49

*Simple flower motif
to embroider in
cross stitch on a
pocket or even a
shopping bag*

48

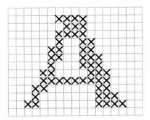
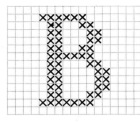
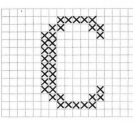

Embroidered purse

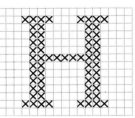
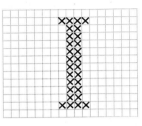
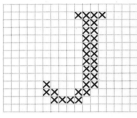

Materials

10 inch by 8 inch strip of evenweave linen, about 19 threads to the inch

Anchor stranded cotton in colours of your choice

7½ inch by 5 inch piece of fabric for lining (Finished purse opened flat measures 6½ inches by 4 inches with a 2½ inch deep pocket)

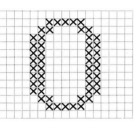
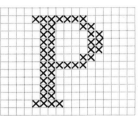
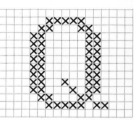

Making up

Work out your design on squared paper, each square representing a stitch. Each cross stitch is worked over two threads on the linen. Position your design on front and back of purse. Make a border all round. The purse pocket can have a name or initials worked on it if desired, and a border across the top.

Having worked your purse, cut out to size allowing ½-inch turnings. Cut out lining and stitch to purse, right sides together, leaving space for turning. Turn to right side, slip stitch opening to close. Turn up and stitch sides of pocket.

Stitch pocket from arrow to arrow

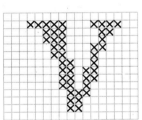
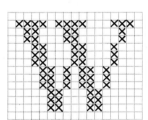
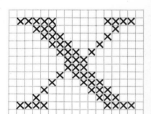

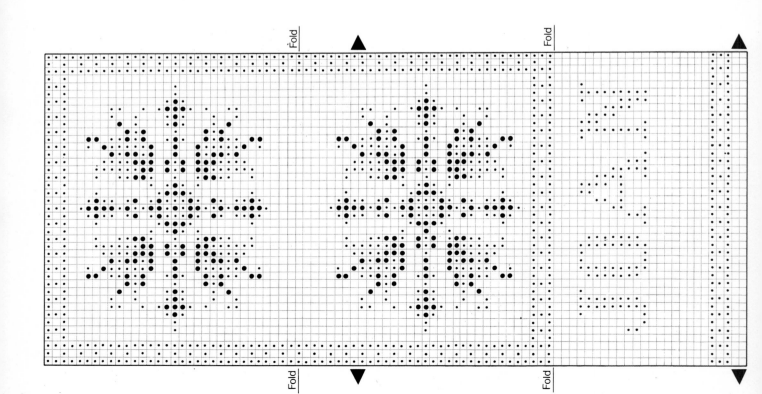

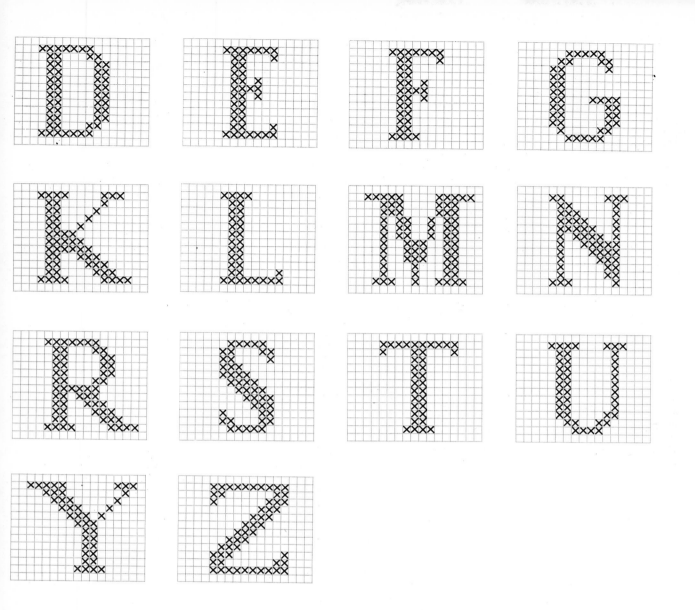

49

Flower motif

Materials
Embroidery silks

Making up
The flower can be embroidered onto an appliqued piece of canvas or worked directly on to a garment. Here the flower has been worked directly, but if you intend to appliqué the patch use a thin fine canvas for a lightweight material such as a blouse, and a thicker canvas for a coarse linen garment such as an apron.

Transfer the design onto the canvas or material—one square on the graph corresponds to one cross stitch. Choose the colours you wish to use and start cross stitching. Start with the lower stitches, working from left to right, going on to the upper stitches working from right to left.

50-51
Dog lead and collar in natural macramé

52-53
Macramé belt and wristband in vivid colours

54-55
Macramé sash and headband decorated with glass beads

Setting on threads

Cut a length of yarn about six inches longer than the finished width of the work. Pin to the top of knotting board with overhand knots so that it is taut and running under the setting on knots.

Cut working threads eight times the length of the finished work. Fold each thread in half and tie onto the foundation thread by holding the doubled strand in front of the foundation thread, fold it over the back and pull the ends through the loop, tightening the knot round the foundation thread. The set on threads are pushed close together and it helps to prevent tangling if each thread is wound into a small ball secured with an elastic band. The thread can then be fed out as it is required.

Diagonal cording

This is worked using one of the knotting threads as a leader, which is held diagonally downwards to either right or left depending on which way the work is intended to slope. The thread next to the leader is knotted round it in a same double knot. Continue along the row until a diagonal bar is formed. Cross leaders in the middle as shown in diagram.

Flat knots

To work flat knots, four threads, or multiples of four, are required. The two centre threads act as a core and the two outer threads are knotted round them. Hold the centre threads taut by winding them round the third finger of the left hand or by securing them to the bottom of the board with a bulldog clip.

Form the right-hand thread into a loop with the end passing under the centre core and over the left-hand thread. Bring the left-hand thread over the core and thread it through the loop from the front of the work. Pull both ends up until the knot closes tightly round the centre core. This completes the first part of the knot.

Repeat the process in reverse by forming the left-hand thread into a loop and passing the right-hand thread through the loop. Draw up tight.

Overhand knot

An overhand knot can be worked with any number of threads. All thicknesses are held together and used as one to form a loop into which the working end is inserted, top to bottom and front to back. The ends are then pulled to tighten the knot.

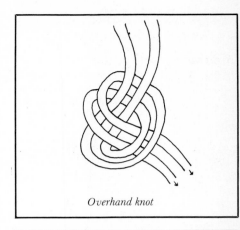

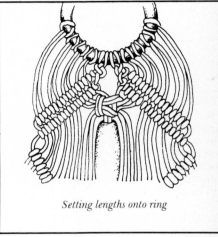

Overhand knot

Setting lengths onto ring

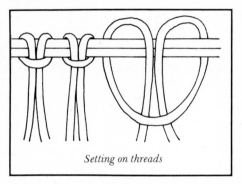

Setting on threads

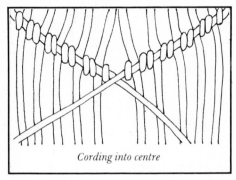

Cording into centre

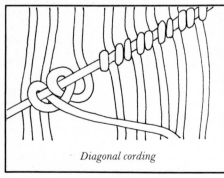

Diagonal cording

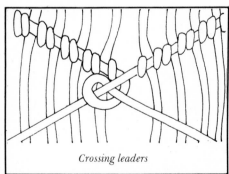

Crossing leaders

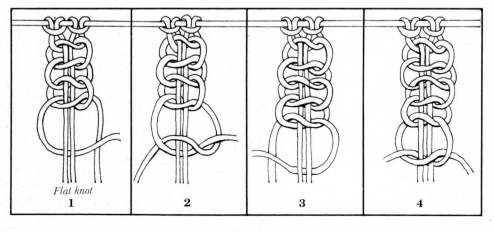

Flat knot

1   2   3   4

50, 51

Macramé dog lead and collar

Materials

26 yards Atlas Cotton Seine Twine
  No. 18 medium
22 yards Atlas Cotton Seine Twine
  No. 18 medium (collar)
One metal dog lead fastener
One gilt buckle, 1 inch by 1½ inch deep,
  with centre spike (collar)
One gilt D-ring (collar)
Adhesive

Measurements

Lead: Length, 30 inches excluding tassel
Width, ½ inch
Tassel, 7 inches
Collar: Length, 15 inches
Width, 1 inch

Making up the lead

Cut two lengths each 11 yards and one length 4 yards, double and set onto ring of fastener with the short lengths in the centre. Using these short lengths as a core work flat knots for 24 inches.

Divide the 6 threads into 2 groups of 3. Using the shorter thread in each group as a core work 6 inches of flat knots on each group.

Make an overhand knot with all 6 threads. Cut tassel to 7 inches and fray out ends.

Making up the collar

Cut 2 lengths each 120 inches, 2 lengths each 60 inches and 2 lengths each 216 inches. Double them, setting on across buckle bar in the following order: one 120 inch length, one 60 inch length, one 216 inch length, one 216 inch length, one 60 inch length and one 120 inch length, so that the spike comes between the two 216 inch lengths in the centre. Divide threads into 2 groups of 6 and, using the 2 centre threads as a core, work 2 flat knots on each group. The flat knots on the left are made with the loop to the left (left threads over core threads first), and the flat knots on the right are made with the loop to the right (right threads over core threads first).

Make an overhand knot with the 4 centre threads (2 from each flat knot). Divide threads into 2 groups of 6. Work one flat knot with the loop to the left, and one flat knot with the loop to the right. Repeat from * to * until there are 11 overhand knots in the centre.

In order to incorporate D-ring, loop the 4 centre threads over the flat side of the D-ring before making the next 3 overhand knots. Repeat from * to * until the collar measures 15 inches.

To finish off

Work 2 flat knots each over 6 threads. Work a flat knot with 4 centre threads. Turn in threads and sew in at the back. Cut and secure with a touch of clear glue.

52,53

Macramé belt and wristband in vivid colours

Materials

1 hank each of pink, purple, green in Atlas Tubular Rayon Cord
Buckle
Small piece Velcro

Measurements

Belt: 26 inches by $1\frac{3}{4}$ inches
Wristband: 8 inches by $1\frac{3}{4}$ inches
Each repeat measure $1\frac{1}{2}$ inches

Making up the belt

Cut 2 pink lengths each 24 inches, 2 purple lengths each 24 inches and 4 green lengths each 15 inches. Set threads on to loop end of buckle as follows: 2 green, one pink, 2 purple, one pink and 2 green.
Using 2nd thread from left as leader, cord diagonally to the left over next thread. Using 15th thread from left, cord diagonally to the right over next thread.
Using 4th thread from left as leader, cord diagonally to the left over next 3 threads. Using 13th thread from left, cord diagonally to the right over next 3 threads.

Using each green thread in turn as leader, cord diagonally to the centre over next 8 threads, beginning with the inner green thread of each set.
Using 4 centre green threads as core, make a flat knot with the 2 green threads on either side. Using each green thread in turn as leader, cord diagonally out to the sides over next 8 threads, beginning with the outer green thread of each set. Using 4 centre purple threads as core, make a flat knot with the 2 pink threads on either side. Using each green thread in turn as leader, cord diagonally into centre as before.
Repeat from * to * 14 times more.
N.B. Adjust length here, allowing 24 inches extra thread for each additional pattern repeat.
Using top right-hand green leaders to continue as leader cord to left over next 4 threads. Using inner left-hand green thread as leader cord diagonally to right over next 3 threads. Using next green thread from right-hand set as leader, cord diagonally to left over next 3 threads. Using next green thread from left-hand set as leader, cord diagonally to right over next 2 threads. Using next green thread from right-hand set as leader, cord diagonally to left over next 2 threads. Using next green thread from left-hand set as leader, cord diagonally to right over next thread. Using next green thread from right-hand set as leader, cord diagonally to left over next thread.
Using 2nd pink thread from left as leader, cord diagonally to right over next thread. Using outer pink thread at right-hand edge as leader, cord diagonally to left over next thread. Using outer pink thread at left-hand edge as leader, cord diagonally over next 2 threads. Sew in ends.

Making up the wristband

Cut 2 pink lengths each 9 inches, 2 purple lengths each 9 inches and 4 green lengths each 8 inches. Set on to green foundation thread as for belt. Work as for belt repeating from * to * 3 times more instead of 14. Complete as for belt.

To finish off

Belt: slot pointed end through buckle bar and stitch in place.
Wristband: sew in ends of foundation thread. Stitch a small piece of Velcro under pointed end and on right side of square end.

54,55

Macramé sash and headband with glass beads

Materials

2 spools Atlas Rayon Stool Twine
One gilt ring $1\frac{3}{4}$ inch diameter
8 30mm glass beads
6 12mm glass beads
12 small glass beads (headband)

Measurements

Sash: to fit 38-inch hip adjustable
Width $3\frac{1}{2}$ inches
Fringe 21 inches
Headband: 22 inches excluding fringe
Width $1\frac{1}{4}$ inches
Fringe 12 inches

Making up the sash

Cut 10 lengths each 192 inches. Set them onto the ring with the knots to the back of the work (see diagram).
*Using 2 centre lengths as leaders cord diagonally out to left and right. Work a second row of cording directly under each one just worked. Using the 2 centre threads as a core, work a flat knot with the 2 threads on either side of the core. Pass the 2 core threads through a large bead. Secure with one flat knot under the bead.
Using the outside thread at each side as leader, cord diagonally into the centre. Work a 2nd row of cording directly under each one just worked.* Repeat from * to * 3 more times, crossing the leaders in the centre of the last 2 rows of diagonal cording. **Cord out horizontally to left and right. Thread a small bead onto the 2 centre threads. Using the outside thread at each side as leader, cord· diagonally into the centre directly under the bead. Cross the leaders.** Repeat from ** to ** twice more.
Tie all threads in an overhand knot $2\frac{1}{2}$ inches below the last row of cording. Trim the ends to 24 inches from the knot and unravel to form a fringe.
N.B. The belt can be adjusted to fit any hip size by omitting or adding pattern repeats as required.
Turn the work and make a second side to correspond with the first.

Making up the headband

Cut 6 lengths each 96 inches and 2 lengths each 144 inches. Cut one length 60 inches of wool or embroidery cotton in a matching colour on which to thread the beads in case the hole is very fine or irregular. ·
Lay out all the threads so that the ends are level at the top and make an overhand knot 12 inches down. Pin each thread to the working surface, placing the bead thread in the centre and the 96 inch threads at each outer edge and the 144 inch threads next to them.
Begin work 4 inches below the overhand knot and using the bead thread as core, make a flat knot with one thread from either side.
Using these 2 threads as leaders, cord diagonally out to right and left. *Using bead thread as a core, work a flat knot with one thread from either side. Thread a bead onto the centre thread and secure with one flat knot. Using the outside threads as leaders, cord diagonally back into the centre, cross the right leader over the left one in the middle and cord diagonally out to the sides again.* Repeat from * to * 11 times but omitting the last diagonal cording out to the sides on the last repeat. Work an overhand knot 4 inches from the work and trim ends to correspond with the other end.

56

Pretty felt flowers to make into a posy to decorate a plain hat

57

Gaily patterned and coloured stones

56
Felt flowers

Materials
Felt remnants
Cotton wool
Fine wire
Crêpe paper (green)
Fabric adhesive
Cotton thread

Making up
Cut out the felt into small ovals or petal shapes. Take a length of wire, about 4 inches (or longer, depending on the length of stem you require), and wind a strip of cotton wool around one end. Place a few petals round the wool, and tie firmly with cotton thread.
Cut the crêpe paper into strips and wind round the wire to make the stem.
Using the fabric adhesive, add the rest of the petals one by one to the few already in place. Moisten the outer edges of the petals and gently bend them outwards for a realistic effect.

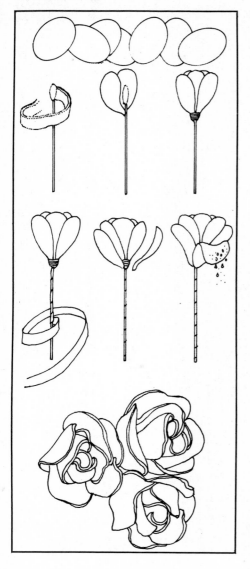

57
Gaily decorated stones

Materials
Suitable smooth, rounded stones
Felt tipped pens in various colours
Clear nail varnish or fixative spray

Making up
First scrub stones clean and dry well. Then carefully draw patterns. Leave stone to dry, then paint with clear nail varnish or spray with fixative (artists use this to prevent drawings from smudging, it does the same for stones but does not make them water-proof).

58
Wool muff

Size
10 inches wide by 16 inches long
Tension
23 sts and 11 rows to 4 inches over patt worked on No. 3·00 (ISR) crochet hook
Materials
Wendy Twinkletwist Tricel Nylon Machine Washable Knit as 4 ply
4 balls each of 5 contrast colours, A, B, C, D and E
One No. 3·00 (ISR) crochet hook

Muff
Using No. 3·00 (ISR) hook and A, make 57ch.
1st row (RS) Using A, into 4th ch from hook work 1tr, *yrh, insert hook into next ch, yrh and draw through loop, yrh and draw through 2 loops on hook, yrh, insert hook into next ch, yrh and draw through loop, yrh and draw through two loops on hook yrh and draw through all loops on hook – called lcl – 1ch, rep from * to last ch, 1tr in last ch. Turn. Join in B.
2nd row Using B, 4ch to count as first tr and 1ch, *lcl into top of next lcl, 1ch, rep from * to end, 1tr into turning ch. Turn.
The 2nd row forms patt and is rep through-out, working in stripes of 1 row C, 1 row D, 1 row E, 1 row A and 1 row B throughout. Cont in patt until work measures 16 inches from beg, ending with a stripe in E. Fasten off.

To make up
Press under a damp cloth with a cool iron.
Cord Cut 3 lengths of each colour 60 inches long. Plait tog.
Fringing Cut rem yarn into 4 inch lengths. Using No. 3·00 (ISR) hook, 3 strands of E each time and with RS of work facing, beg at cast off edge and knot fringe into each lcl and 1ch along row. Keeping colours correct, work in same way along each row. With RS facing, join cast on edge to cast off edge. Keeping seam at lower edge, join each side 3 inches up from lower edge. Turn work to RS. Thread cord through muff opening and knot ends tog.

American readers
A 3·00 (ISR) crochet hook is the equivalent of F. Bernat.
English crochet terms are one step 'ahead' of American terms. See conversion chart below.

ENGLISH	US
single crochet or slip stitch (ss)	slip stitch (sl st)
double crochet (dc)	single crochet (sc)
treble crochet (tr)	double crochet (dc)
half treble (htr)	half double crochet
double treble (dtr)	treble crochet (tr)
triple treble (tr tr)	double treble (dtr)
quadruple treble	triple treble (tr tr)
treble round treble	double round treble
treble between treble	double between double

59

Silky, soft scarves to dye yourself with batik printing

Materials

For waxing you will need:

A double saucepan for melting wax (or a saucepan and a tin to contain the wax, which can be placed in the pan)

A gas ring or electric hotplate – standing on a piece of asbestos if possible, as a safety precaution

Wax, in the form of domestic candles or blocks of paraffin wax purchased from chemists and specialist craft shops. (Powdered wax is also available. Beeswax, which is more expensive, provides the most flexible wax.)

Artists' brushes for applying wax – medium-sized for outlining areas, large-sized for filling in large areas

Tjanting tool

Resin powder

Old picture frame

Drawing pins

A flat table surface

Quantity of old newspaper

For dyeing:

A plastic or enamel bowl to hold the dye mixture

A plastic or glass measure, for water

Rubber gloves

Polythene sheeting, to protect table while dyed material dries

Plastic spoons of various sizes, for spooning out dyes

Small plastic containers for mixing dyes

Cold water dyes

Protective clothing

Nylon clothes line and clothes pegs

Making up

Best results are obtained on cotton, cotton lawn, calico, silk and linen, also on mixtures of wool and cotton. Man-made fibres and materials with special finishes, such as crease-resistant, non-iron or drip-dry fabrics, are not suitable for beginners as the dyes do not penetrate these surfaces easily.

Some very effective patterns can be made by designs based on the circle, the square or the triangle. Natural objects such as stones, shells, bark, seeds, leaves and plants all offer a starting point and the designs will develop almost on their own as the dyeing and waxing progresses.

Preparing for waxing: Before dyeing, the cloth must be washed thoroughly to remove all traces of dressing, sizes and natural oils. When the material is ironed free of creases, it is ready for the application of wax resist.

Preparing the wax: Cut up or grate the candles or pieces cut from a block of wax and melt in a double saucepan over heat. It

should be emphasized that when handling hot wax great care must be taken at all times. A more flexible, less brittle wax is obtained by adding one part of resin to four parts of paraffin wax.

Applying the wax: The wax must be kept hot while you are working and there are two basic methods of applying it. It can be painted on, using a brush, varying the size according to the area to be waxed. For fine lines and for textured effects, a tjanting is used.

There are two ways of working when applying wax. The material can be simply spread out flat on layers of newspaper, and this is the method used when large areas of fabric are being treated. As the wax passes through the fabric, it cools and adheres to the paper beneath. As the fabric is peeled off for dying, the wax inevitably cracks and this can cause the dye to bleed, which may not be part of the design. Beginners will probably find it more satisfactory to work with the fabric pinned to a frame. An old picture frame will do.

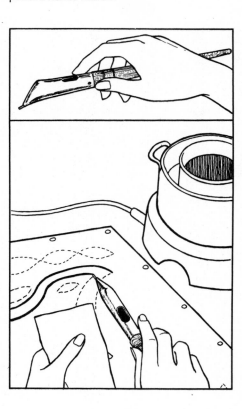

The tjanting is dipped into the hot wax, filling the reservoir, and is then carried to the prepared fabric. To prevent the wax from dripping hold a piece of paper under the spout. Hold the tjanting in the right hand immediately above the surface of the fabric and move it along the design lines. Providing the wax is hot enough, a fine trail of wax will flow from the spout. As the wax penetrates the fabric appears to go transparent. Remember, wax is applied only to those areas which are not going to be dyed.

Batik dyeing: The secret of successful batik dyeing is a large enough container, so that the waxed fabric can be moved around without undue crushing.

Follow the manufacturers' instructions for preparing the dye, and make sure that the solution is quite cool before starting to dye or the wax will melt and destroy the design. If the wax is cracked the dye will run in, and a fine marbling texture will result. This effect is sometimes used for background to designs.

After dyeing is completed, drain the fabric off by laying it flat on several sheets of newspaper spread on a table top. Polythene sheeting under the newspaper will prevent any dye from staining through to the table top. After it has drained, the fabric can be hung up to dry. It is then ready for waxing further areas of the design.

After two applications of wax and dye, boil off the wax and start again. This is very important because dye chemicals cause a deterioration in the wax and dye can penetrate the fabric in areas which should be free of dye.

This process of waxing and cold dyeing is repeated until as many colours have been applied as required.

Removing the wax: There are two methods of removing wax. The first is by boiling the wax out of the fabric. Heat the water in a large saucepan and when the water is boiling put in the waxed fabric. Gently move it about with a wooden spoon for not more than three minutes.

Lift the fabric out and drop it into a bucket of cold water. The wax will solidify immediately. After squeezing out the water, shake off the loose wax. Add half a teaspoonful of detergent to the boiling water and repeat this process twice, or until there is no trace of wax left. Finally, wash and dry the fabric (professional dry cleaning will remove the residue).

Waxy water must never be poured down a sink, as it will cause a blockage. Wait until the water cools, then remove the crust of wax on the surface of the water and pour the clear water away. The wax cannot be used again because the dye chemicals have probably deteriorated it.

Points to watch: The technique of batik printing is straightforward, but while you are learning you may experience one or two disappointments. Here are some points to watch to help you to achieve the best results.

Bleeding of colour under the wax. This can happen if the wax is not hot enough to penetrate the fabric, or if the wax is damaged as the waxed fabric is pulled off the newspaper. It is best to use a frame.

Blurred edges to the design. This will result if the dye solution is warm and the waxed design softened. Make sure the dye is cool.

Blurred designs and muddied colours. This will result if the fabric is left to boil too long when boiling out the wax. The loose dye in the water can be re-absorbed.

Pale colours. If the dye is not sufficiently fixed before the wax is boiled off, the colour may wash out and be too pale. Allow the dye to dry thoroughly first. If you are not pleased with the result of waxing and dyeing, the majority of cold dyes can be removed by boiling the fabric in a solution of colour remover.

59

Batik dyeing

Above and opposite: two simple designs for the beginner to use for a basic two-colour batik scarf, using the natural fabric colour and a contrasting coloured dye. The designs are 6 inches square.
Left: the dye colours the fabric which has not been waxed, reversing the pattern.
Right: the finished scarf has the motifs positioned alternately for an interesting contrast effect.

60

Jewellery housewife

Materials

½ yard 36-inch wide taffeta
¼ yard wadding
About ½ yard embroidered ribbon, 3½ to
    4 inches wide
½ yard baby ribbon
Matching thread

Making up

The finished size of this jewellery housewife when opened out is about 6 inches by 12 inches. Use a rich looking piece of fabric for the right side or decorate it with embroidered ribbon or braid. The folder is lined and interlined with wadding; the pockets are also interlined. Fasten with ties of ribbon.

Cut out two pieces of fabric, each 7 inches by 13 inches for top and lining. Cut three strips of the lining fabric for pockets at the end and sides, each measuring 7 inches square, 7 inches by 5 inches and 7 inches by 8 inches. ½-inch seams allowed throughout. Cut out four pieces of wadding for interlining, measuring respectively 6 inches by 12 inches, 3 inches by 6 inches, 2 inches by 6 inches and 3½ inches by 6 inches.

With right sides together, stitch the side seams of pockets. Trim seams. Turn to right side and insert interlining (diagram 1). Tack the interlining to the wrong side of lining piece. Position pockets on right side of lining as shown in diagram 2. Stitch these to the lining at sides and with running stitches catch down centre of lining to wadding. Tack down end pocket at sides. Place the embroidered ribbon centrally on the top piece and stitch. The top can also be made from a 7 inch by 13 inch piece of patterned fabric.

With right sides together, sew the lining to the top fabric on three sides. Trim edges and corners, turn to right side and press lightly. Turn in the ends and slip stitch together. Roll up and position the baby ribbon ties for fastening. Sew the ribbon on.

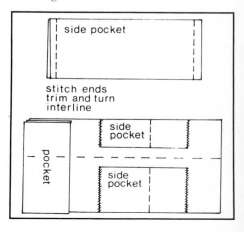

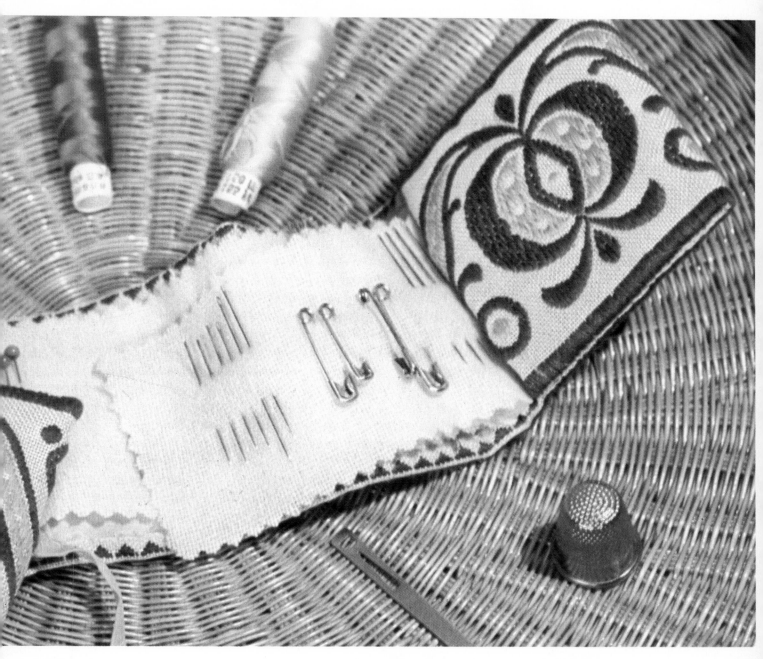

61

Spectacles case

Materials

Two rectangles of buckram about $5\frac{3}{4}$ inches by $2\frac{3}{4}$ inches or to required finished size
Two pieces of outer fabric or braid
Two strips of lining fabric to cover buckram plus $\frac{1}{2}$-inch seam allowances.

Making up

Round off the corners of the buckram rectangles. Cover the outer sides of buckram with fabric and then line these pieces, turning in edges of fabric and lining. Slip stitch together.

Oversew the two sections together at sides and bottom, leaving the top open from curved corners.

62

Sewing housewife

Materials

$\frac{1}{2}$ yard braid or woven ribbon, 3 inches wide
$\frac{1}{2}$ yard ribbon or strip of fabric for lining
Strip of flannel, 3 inches by 16 inches long
$\frac{1}{2}$ yard narrow ribbon or press stud
Pinking shears

Making up

Line the strip of braid or ribbon and neaten ends. Fold up ends to make two pockets, one $2\frac{1}{2}$ inches deep and the other $1\frac{1}{2}$ inches deep. Pink the edges of flannel and fold in half lengthwise. Sew the fold to the lining of the housewife. Fill with needles, silks and pins. Roll housewife up and attach ribbon or press stud to fasten.

63

Fragrant lavender bags

Materials
Oddments of fabric – cotton, lace, voile
Ribbon and decorative trimming
Dried lavender

Making up
Cut the fabric into the shape required, hearts, circles or rectangles.

To make the square bag, fold a rectangle in half with the right sides together and stitch the two sides. Hem the remaining raw edges. Turn the bag right side out and press. Fill with lavender, and tie the opening with length of ribbon.

To make the more decorative shapes, cut two pieces of fabric to shape required, place right sides together and stitch, leaving a 2-inch space for turning. Turn right side out, press and fill with lavender. Turn in the raw edges of the opening and slip stitch together. Slip stitch lace, ribbon or decoration in place.

To dry your own lavender, cut when in full flower early in the morning before the sun has reached it. Tie into bunches and leave to dry in the sun for three to four weeks. When dry shake the lavender heads free from the stems.

64

Subtle pot pourri mixture in lacy sachets

Materials
Pot pourri mixture:
A collection of sweet scented flowers: rosebuds, lavender, stock, lemon verbena, rosemary, thyme, pinks, honeysuckle, mint and bay leaves
$\frac{1}{4}$ lb. each of common salt (non-iodized), brown sugar, coarse salt
$\frac{1}{2}$ oz. each of nutmeg, cinnamon, ground cloves, allspice, gum benzoin, borax, ground orris root
(Optional:
1 cup each of orange and lemon peel, well pounded)
Wire cake trays for drying petals
Tightly stoppered jar
Sachets:
Wide meshed net or curtain lace or medallions of old lace
Fine net or organdie for lining

Making up pot pourri
Dry flower petals by spreading them over wire trays which allow plenty of air to circulate. Keep in a dark place for two to three weeks.

Make up the spice mixture. When petals are ready, place a layer of petals in the jar, then a layer of spice mixture. Continue alternating layers to the top.

Tightly close the jar and keep for two or three days, then mix thoroughly. Replace stopper. Continue stirring frequently during the next two to three weeks.

When ready put mixture in sachets or pretty china pots.

Making up sachet

Choose a pretty shape, cut two pieces and slip stitch together round the edge, leave an opening for filling. Line with fine net. Slip stitch to close.

If you want to fill the bags with lavender, make the inner sachet from organdie, so that the lavender does not fall through. You can dye or paint the lace or leave it the natural colour. Finish with a ribbon tie or edge with ruching.

65

Arrangement of dried flowers and grasses

Materials

Dried flowers, leaves, dyed grasses, fir cones, plastic fruit and flowers
A smooth stick about 12 to 13 inches long
Florist's wire
Ribbon

Making up

Begin from the top of the stick and work downwards. Bind the grasses, flowers and so on around the stick using the florist's wire.

Wind the decorative ribbon round the centre of the stick and secure with a bow.